101

Facts About Queen Victoria

By

Joanne Hayle.

Young Victoria

Princess Victoria of Kent aged 4.

1. Victoria was born on 24th May 1819 at
    Kensington Palace in London. It was a chilly
    morning, an hour or so before dawn. During

the Georgian era, Kensington was only used by minor royals and parts of the palace had steadily fallen in to disrepair. It was not the glorious royal abode we recognise today.

2. Victoria was the only legitimate child of Edward, Duke of Kent, the 4th son of George III and Queen Charlotte. Her mother, Victoire, was the widow of Emich Karl, 2nd Prince of Leiningen. She already had two children, Karl and Feodora of Leiningen.

3. Victoire was the sister of Leopold of Saxe Coburg Saalfeld, the widower of Princess Charlotte Augusta of Wales, the Prince Regent's daughter, late heir to the throne.

4. Victoria's esteemed Uncle Leopold, a dashing soldier of fortune, later became King of the Belgians. Over the years he actively steered Victoria towards her cousin Prince Albert of Saxe Coburg Gotha, one of his nephews.

5. When Princess Charlotte and her infant son passed away after a strenuous labour in November 1817, there were no legitimate heirs for the thrones of Britain and Hanover. There were up to 22 illegitimate offspring by George III's sons, but all were ineligible to take a place in the succession. This was a significant crisis for the House of Hanover. George III was in failing health and handled no matters of state after 1811, but Queen Charlotte was clear about what she expected: The Prince Regent's dissolute unmarried brothers must set aside their mistresses and do their duty; marry, have issue and save the dynasty's fortunes.

6. Queen Victoria's father had kept a mistress, Julie, full name Madame Alphonsine-Thérèse-Bernardine-Julie de Montgenêt de Saint-Laurent and for twenty-eight years they lived as if married. He turned away from her, much to her distress, to fulfil his duty. She retired to Paris, France where she lived quietly until her death in 1830.

7. Victoria's parents were married at Schloss Ehrenburg in Coburg on 29 May 1818. On 11th July 1818 there was a double wedding at Kew for the Kent's and the Duke of Clarence (later King William IV) and his bride Adelaide of Saxe-Meiningen. Formalities were carried out in the dying Queen Charlotte's presence.

8. The Duke and Duchess of Kent were forced to live modestly. Like most of his brothers, Edward consistently lived beyond his means and economies had to be introduced to pay his substantial debts.

9. Adolphus, Duke of Cambridge's wife Augusta bore a boy, George, on 26th March 1819, in Hanover. Edward and Victoire welcomed Victoria on 24th May 1819. Frederica, Duchess of Cumberland, bore her son George on 27th May 1819 in Berlin. The Kent's had been careful to ensure that their child was born on British soil to strengthen his or her "Britishness."

10. Although Prince George of Cambridge was the eldest of the three, in the line of

succession Kent sat before Cumberland and Cambridge so Victoria "won" the baby race. At this point there was still a chance that Victoire would bear a son and displace Victoria under the rule of primogeniture. Fate decreed otherwise.

11. She was 5th in line to the throne at her birth. George III was still alive, the Prince Regent, Duke of York, Duke of Clarence and her father, Duke of Kent were ahead of Victoria in the line of succession.

12. We came to know her as Victoria, but she was named Alexandrina Victoria. In her infancy she was known as Drina. When it became clear that she was destined to reign, Drina became Victoria, in private and then public; it was deemed a much more suitable name for a British monarch.

13. For the first few years of her life, Drina spoke only German. It was when she became "Victoria" that she learned English as a first language.

14. Alexandrina was chosen as a Christian name because her parents had an acrimonious relationship with the Duke's brother, George, the Prince Regent, and he had refused permission for her to be named in his honour. Victoire's sister Juliane had married in to the Russian Romanov dynasty and Alexander I, Tsar of Russia was chosen as a godfather. Rumour had it that the use of the Tsar's name for their daughter was a reminder to George that he was not all powerful, there were other rulers of vast empires in the world.

15. She was christened at Kensington Palace in the Cupola Room by Charles Manners-Sutton, the Archbishop of Canterbury.

16. Victoria's father died of pneumonia on 23rd January 1820 in an economically priced and damp Woolbrook Cottage in Sidmouth, Devon; the reduction in spending cost the family dearly. Less than a year after her birth, the *little may flower* was fatherless and Victoire had three children to care for.

17. In widowhood, little provision was made for
    Victoire by her detested brother in law, the
    Prince Regent. She was given accommodation
    at Kensington Palace and received some
    money from the civil list. Parliament
    remembered the sum of accrued debts that
    the Duke had left and restricted her annuity
    accordingly.

18. George IV found his niece delightful and
    welcomed her warmly to his homes for visits.
    Not so the Duchess of Kent.

19. When Victoria first met her uncle William,
    Duke of Clarence (from 1830, King William
    IV) at Windsor, he put her at her ease by
    instructing her to "Give me your little paw."
    He also presented her with his portrait set in
    diamonds.

20. Victoire, as a lonely and isolated foreigner felt
    vulnerable. The comptroller of her household,
    Sir John Conroy, capitalised on this and
    manipulated her so that he held the true
    decision-making powers and kept her, and
    Victoria, away from external influences. His

ultimate goal was to be the power behind the throne if Victoria became queen whilst still a minor. A Victoire headed regency until Victoria's 18th birthday effectively meant that he would be in charge and his grandiose ambitions achieved. He also ingratiated himself with the near blind Princess Sophia, daughter of George III, spent her money and used her to spy for him.

21. Victoria was Conroy's passport to glory, but he could be cruel to her. Victoire, perhaps out of desperation, refused to see his faults. She agreed that her daughter was foolish and frivolous and that even as an adult she would require his advice.

22. The oppressive Kensington system, which protected Victoria from harm at the hands of her unscrupulous Hanoverian uncles, was detested by her. She could not use the stairs unassisted and was rarely left alone; she shared a bedroom with her mother and her food would be tasted to ensure that it had not been tampered with.

23. Conroy increased Victoire's worries about Victoria's safety by using the Duke of Cumberland's history and the claim that his son Prince George had, as next in line of succession after Victoria, to ensure that the Kensington system was not neglected and Victoire's paranoia was maintained. The Duke of Cumberland had long been suspected of murdering his valet. He was also suspected of raping his sister, Princess Sophia. (The princess Sir John Conroy used for personal advancement.) His wife, Duchess Frederica may have evaded the red tape of divorce by killing her second husband Prince Frederick William of Solms-Braunfels so that she could marry Cumberland. Prince Frederick's death was deemed too convenient for many commentators. Rightly or wrongly. in the public's eye, the Cumberland's were shocking villains.

24. Victoria's governess Baroness Louise Lehzen, known as Daisy, was her true champion. She was regarded as a mother figure by Victoria and Lehzen cultivated her charge's independence and inner personal strength to

combat Conroy and Victoire's efforts. Born Johanna Clara Louise Lehzen on 3rd October 1784 in Hanover, as one of the younger daughters of a Lutheran pastor she was destined to earn her living as a governess. She joined the Kent household in late 1819 as a governess to Princess Feodora of Leiningen and then Victoria. Lehzen was a clever woman, underestimated by Conroy who'd initially assumed that she would accommodate his wishes without question.

25. Looking back, Victoria spoke of her early years as utterly miserable, but in truth she was happy overall. Her memories were tainted by negative episodes featuring Sir John Conroy and her mother.

26. Victoria learned to stay within budget when she started to receive pocket money; almost a unique quality for members of the House of Hanover!

27. In 1832 Victoria first wrote her journal, a habit that she retained until ten days before her death in 1901. *"This book, Mamma gave*

me, that I might write the journal of my journey to Wales in it. Victoria. Kensington Palace. July 31st." The journey commenced the next day. Her juvenile entries were frequently read by her mother. Her last journal entry on 13th January 1901 was from Osborne House on the Isle of Wight. Her youngest daughter, Beatrice noted the following to conclude volume 111, *"This is the last entry into the Queen's Journal before her death on Jan: 22nd."* The combined number of words written from 1832 to 1901 exceeds 60 million.

28. Victoria's artistic gifts were noted; she was adept at sketching and painting from an early age and throughout her life she embraced art. As she grew up she read Charles Dickens, and her dancing and musical skills were accomplished.

29. As a child, her feared uncle Ernest, Duke of Cumberland, gave Victoria a parrot named Lory. King Victor Emmanuel of Italy gifted her two Shetland ponies, Alma and Flora but

her favourite, and most well- known, pet was Dash, a King Charles spaniel.

30. Victoria learned of her proximity to the throne when she was twelve years old. Upon hearing the news, she commented "I will be good."

31. When on holiday in Ramsgate, Kent, 16 year old Victoria fell ill with a serious fever. Conroy, apparently with Victoire's agreement, at first dismissed the fever as childish behaviour and then took the opportunity to bully Victoria in to making him her official private secretary. Dramatic scenes ensued, but Victoria refused to comply.

32. During adolescence Victoria grew to approximately 4 feet 11 inches and her clothes were attractive, stately and tiny. The Hanoverians were prone to weight gain and her grief about losing Prince Albert increased her form considerably from late 1861 onwards. A pair of her bloomers from the 1890's has a 50 inch waist.

33. It was 20th June 1837 at 6a.m. that Victoria learned that her uncle William IV had passed away and that she was Queen Victoria. The public proclamation was made at St. James Palace at 10a.m. the same day.

34. She was eighteen years old so there was no need for a regency. King William IV despised Conroy and disliked the Duchess of Kent; he had stated that, despite his indifferent health, he would endeavour to live until Victoria could rule in her own right. He died within weeks of her reaching adulthood.

William IV circa early 1837, by one of his 10
illegitimate children, Sophia Sidney,
Baroness De L'isle and Dudley. She was his
eldest daughter and State Housekeeper of

Kensington Palace. She died in childbirth in April 1837. The king was heartbroken.

35. Victoria was unable to reign in Hanover because the country followed Salic Law, a male only line of succession. She dispatched the Duke of Cumberland, her heir presumptive until she bore children, to Hanover where he ruled until his death in November 1851. His son George succeeded him and ruled until his first cousin Wilhelm dethroned him as part of Germany's unification in 1866.

36. One of the queen's first acts in what became known as the Victorian era, was to shatter Sir John Conroy's dreams for power. She made it clear that she had no need for him in her household, in her government or even in Britain. He presented a list of demands; Victoria agreed to a pension of £3000 per annum but she refused him an Irish peerage to add to his British one.

37. Victoire couldn't understand why Victoria was being so ungrateful to Sir John Conroy after all his labours on her behalf, and she retained him in her household until 1839 when the Duke of Wellington persuaded Conroy to leave the Duchess and travel with his family. In 1842 Conroy retired to his Berkshire estate, accrued debts and passed away in March 1854. After his death, Victoire had checked her historic financial accounts and found that significant funds had apparently been siphoned off by Conroy during his tenure.

38. Victoria was the first monarch to reside at Buckingham Palace. Her income included revenues from the Duchies of Cornwall and Lancaster; Each monarch since Victoria, including Elizabeth II, has received the title the *Duke* of Lancaster. Victoria didn't like the term Duchess and felt that only men should hold this rank in society.

39. Victoria used some of the money she received from the Civil List to pay off her father's outstanding debts.

40. The new queen's cousin Prince Albert of Saxe Coburg Gotha, who she'd met in 1836, wrote a letter of congratulations to her stating that, *"In your hand lies the happiness of millions."*

41. Victoria distanced herself from her mother, giving her (and Conroy) suites of rooms at the far end of the palace. They barely communicated. Her uneasy relationship with her mother remained until the Duchess' illness and death in 1861 but it became less fractious after the birth of a grandchild, Princess Victoria in 1840.

42. Queen Victoria's coronation was held on 28th June 1838 at Westminster Abbey. When the aptly named courtier Sir John Rolle climbed the steps to the dais to pay homage to her he fell and rolled down the steps. She made her way from the cloth of gold covered throne, off the dais and down a step so that he could reach her without further incident. It was an act of kindness that won her admiration.

43. Until she was queen, Victoria didn't have a coat of arms, a heraldic sign which denotes lineage and achievements. She then had two created for her, one for use in the United Kingdom and another for use in Great Britain and Northern Ireland. The second is preferred in Scotland.

44. Victoria was under pressure from the establishment to marry but she resisted. Whig leader Lord Melbourne, her first Prime Minister, was like a kind uncle to her. He helped her to navigate her way through the demanding responsibilities which filled her days.

William Lamb, 2ⁿᵈ Viscount Melbourne.
Victoria's "Dear Lord M." circa 1844.

45. Lord Melbourne quickly became indispensable to Victoria, and throughout her life she seems to have needed, or at least appreciated, having a strong male by her side from Dear Lord M. and Prince Albert to John Brown and Abdul Karim, the Munshi, her favourite Indian servant.

46. The young Queen Victoria's worst errors of judgement occurred in 1839. One of the

Duchess of Kent's unmarried ladies in waiting, Lady Flora Hastings, was suffering from a swelling around her abdomen. Rumours flew about the court that she was pregnant with Sir John Conroy's child. Flora's known dislike for Baroness Lehzen, her compliance with the detested Conroy and the Kensington System meant that Victoria, Lord Melbourne, Sir James Clark, the court physician, the Whig politicians and the court gossips eagerly vilified Flora. Meanwhile, the Tory politicians, the Hastings and Conroy families mounted a counter campaign in the press. This swayed public opinion against Victoria, Dr. Clark and Lord Melbourne. Public sympathy rested securely with Lady Flora. Pressurised into having a medical examination, Flora was found to be a virgin; the salacious rumours were entirely false. Flora had a tumour on her liver which, as it had developed, steadily distorted her abdomen. A penitent Queen Victoria visited Flora on 27th June to make peace with her. Lady Flora Hastings died aged 33 on 5th July 1839.

47. In May 1839, Whig Prime Minister Lord Melbourne told Victoria that he intended to resign. She was faced with a new Prime Minister, the Tory Robert Peel, which traditionally meant a change of her ladies of the bedchamber to ladies aligned with the political party in power. The Queen favoured the Whigs, she was happy to have Whig ladies attending her and so she refused to comply. Her standoff with Peel caused the "Bedchamber Crisis." Peel refused to form a government until Victoria agreed to Tory ladies of the bedchamber. At a stalemate, Melbourne returned as Prime Minister until August 1841. Support for Peel had steadily increased over the 2 years, and it was made clear to the queen that her personal preference must be sacrificed for the good of the country; she should do what was expected of her. Begrudgingly, she accepted Peel as Prime Minister and appointed Tory ladies. After this struggle, Victoria grew quite fond of Peel.

Victoria and Albert

Queen Victoria and Prince Albert circa 1854.

48. The suggestion of a union between Princess Victoria of Kent and Prince Albert of Saxe Coburg Gotha was first written about in 1821 by Augusta, the Dowager Duchess of Saxe Coburg Saalfeld, the maternal grandmother of Victoria and the paternal grandmother of Albert.

49. Albert Francis Charles Augustus Emmanuel of Saxe Coburg Gotha was born on 26 August 1819 at Schloss Rosenau. He was the second son and last child of Ernst I, Duke of Saxe Coburg Gotha and his wife Louise of Saxe Coburg Altenburg. It was a tempestuous marriage and Ernst I had double standards when it came to adultery. He felt that he could do whatever he wanted, but when he learned that Louise was having an affair in 1824 he banished her, and they were divorced. When it was discovered that she had secretly married her lover, Baron Alexander von Hanstein, she was denied access to her sons. She never saw them again. Louise died of cancer in France aged 30.

50. Albert was extremely studious and well behaved. He followed a strict dawn to dusk schedule of learning. His brother Ernst, born in 1818, was less academic and as an adult he followed in his father's footsteps to become a noted philanderer. Albert's male dominated

upbringing made him awkward with most females, except Victoria.

51. The two children grew up assuming they would marry each other one day. By the time of Victoria and Albert's first meeting in 1836, their uncle Leopold, the king of the Belgians (widower of Princess Charlotte of Wales) was confidently nudging Victoria towards viewing Albert as her future husband.

52. King William IV had favoured Prince Alexander of the Netherlands, the second son of the Prince of Orange, as Victoria's future husband. She thought that Alexander was plain, but that Albert of Saxe Coburg Gotha was handsome, and she enjoyed his company. Prince Alexander died of tuberculosis whilst living on the island of Madeira, aged 29 and unmarried.

53. The idea of a marriage between Victoria and Prince George of Cumberland was suggested but neither party was keen. George looked quite like Prince Albert, but George and

Victoria grew up as first cousins and they couldn't consider the other as a spouse.

54. Queen Victoria proposed to Albert and they were married on the 10th February 1840. She recorded the day in her journal. *"His beauty, his sweetness and gentleness, really how can I ever be thankful enough to have such a Husband!"* Unromantically, on the wedding night, Victoria felt unwell. Happily, after she'd vomited, she rallied, and they consummated the marriage. On 11th February she wrote: *"When day dawned (for we did not sleep much) and I beheld that beautiful angelic face by my side, it was more than I can express!"*

55. Albert was determined not to have a failed marriage like his parents. Morality was his watchword and under his influence Victoria became less fun loving and more reserved.

56. Under the tutelage of doctor-statesman-advisor Baron Stockmar and King Leopold, Albert was taught how to become

indispensable to Victoria. He learned his lessons well.

57. After a series of arguments about Victoria's imperious nature, Albert's purpose in Britain and the powerful influence of Victoria's governess turned advisor Baroness Lehzen, it became evident that either Albert or the Baroness must leave Victoria's side. Lehzen and Albert were never fond of one another, they competed for supremacy in Victoria's life. Lehzen had voiced her reluctance before the wedding to seeing Victoria married to her Saxe Coburg Gotha cousin, stating that she should be a virgin queen like the Tudor Elizabeth I. Albert referred to Lehzen as "the hag" and averred that she was a "crazy stupid intriguer," unworthy of Victoria's favour. She, in his view, had risen above her station in life. Victoria conceded to her husband's wishes after an altercation about the care of their first child, Vicky, and Lehzen was dismissed. To soften the blow, she was awarded a substantial pension. The baroness returned home to Hanover where she lived out her remaining days. Victoria visited her when she

made trips to Germany and Lehzen corresponded with her until her death in 1870 aged 85. Baron Stockmar, Albert's advisor, recorded that: *"She was foolish enough to contest his [Albert's] influence, and not to conform herself to the change in her position."*

58. The passionate Victoria loathed the inevitable pregnancies that resulted from her marriage; she viewed them as "occupational hazards." The queen was never fond of babies, including her own. She commented that: *"An ugly baby is a very nasty object – and the prettiest is frightful."*

Victoria with her eldest daughter. Mid 1840's.

59. Victoria and Albert's first child, Victoria
    Adelaide Mary Louisa, was born on 21st
    November 1840. She was her father's
    favourite. Betrothed aged 14, at 17, she

married Prince Friedrich of Prussia. They had eight children, two died in infancy. For decades, Vicky was unfairly vilified by most Prussians including her eldest son Willy, Kaiser Wilhelm II, the man who led Europe in to World War I in 1914, for being British. Cancer stricken, she lived for less than eight months after her mother's 1901 death.

Albert Edward was born on the 9th November 1841. He was known as Bertie. His parents had unrealistic expectations; Victoria wanted a replica of perfect Prince Albert and the implementation of a harsh regime, endless study and almost constant criticism left a legacy. As an adult he took full advantage of freedoms including gambling and sexual adventures, he had numerous mistresses including Alice Keppel and Lillie Langtry. Bertie detested being bored or unoccupied. Whilst Queen Victoria hated Bertie's pleasure-seeking lifestyle she gave him no work to do, thereby perpetuating the problem. Queen Victoria blamed Bertie for Prince Albert's death in 1861; she believed that the stress of Bertie's liaison with actress and good time girl Nellie Clifden weakened Albert's resistance to illness. Bertie succeeded his mother and reigned as King Edward VII between 1901-1910, with more success than his mother could ever have imagined.

Alice Maud Mary followed on 25th April 1843. After her marriage, as Grand Duchess of Hesse and By Rhine, she had the rare distinction of angering her mother so much by choosing to breastfeed her children that Queen Victoria named a cow in the dairy after her. Alice invited intellectuals, who challenged the status quo, to her home in Darmstadt which did not meet with Queen Victoria's approval; scolding letters were frequently received by Alice. She died on the 17th anniversary of her father's death on 14th December 1878. Her best- known child was Alix; Tsarina Alexandra Feodorovna of Russia, who was assassinated with her husband Tsar Nicholas II and their children in Yekaterinburg on 17th July 1918.

Alfred Ernest Albert, Affie to his family, born 6th August 1844 was similar to Bertie in nature. He too was criticised for not being flawless, to the extent that when he went on an official tour of Australia in March 1868 and was almost assassinated, his account of the shooting and his relief at being alive were damned by Victoria. Far from being delighted that her son hadn't been killed she asserted her opinion that he had made the story of the failed assassination all about himself, and he wasn't nearly thankful or humble enough to have been spared.

Affie enjoyed his naval career but found that his later life as the Duke of Saxe Coburg Gotha and in a loveless marriage to Maria Alexandrovna of Russia offered him a stultifying existence which wasted his talents. Consequently, he drank too much. His son and heir, Alfred, died on 6th February 1899 and Affie followed in 1900, suffering from cancer and heartbroken. The Duchess of Saxe Coburg Gotha was blamed for the son Alfred's death; he tried to commit suicide during a scandal and whilst his life lay in the balance she chose to have him moved from Gotha to

Merano in Italy, against medical advice, and the journey proved fatal.

Affie and Maria's four daughters married into European houses.

Helena Augusta Victoria, "Lenchen" 1846-1923 was next. She married Prince Christian of Schleswig-Holstein in 1866; he had the title but not the land as Prussia had fought and won a war for the territories in 1864. The couple lived in Britain. Helena is noted for being dedicated to carrying out public engagements and was the founding president of the Royal School of Needlework, of the Workhouse Infirmary Nursing Association and the Royal British Nurses' Association. She campaigned for women's rights against her mother's wishes.

Their eldest son, Christian, born in 1867, died in the Boer War; second son Albert inherited the Schleswig-Holstein title but never married or had legitimate issue.

The couple's two daughters Helena Victoria and Marie Louise were nicknamed "the princesses of nowhere" after they surrendered their overseas titles for British ones in 1917 as a sign of patriotism. Two more children were born; Harald died at eight days old in May 1876 and an unnamed stillborn son arrived in May 1877.

In 1916, Helena and Christian became the first members of her family to celebrate their 50th wedding anniversary.

Louise Caroline Alberta, born in 1848, was an acclaimed sculptor; the statue of Queen Victoria in Kensington Palace Gardens is Louise's work. She was a patron of the arts, had a modern liberal outlook, was forthright and a renowned feminist. The only child of Queen Victoria and Prince Albert to marry a commoner and to have no children, her marriage to John Campbell, then Marquess of Lorne, gave her freedom from her mother. Louise had acted as Victoria's unofficial private secretary from the time of Helena's marriage in 1866 and by 1870 she wanted marriage and her own household.

John and Louise became the 9th Duke and Duchess of Argyll in 1900.

Called *Auntie Palace* by the young princesses Elizabeth and Margaret of York, (Elizabeth is the present queen) Louise died in 1939, aged 91, at Kensington Palace.

Arthur William Patrick Albert, 1850-1942, was a born soldier. On his mother's birthday in 1874 he was created Duke of Connaught and Strathern, Earl of Sussex. He married Louise of Prussia and when in England they lived at Bagshot Park, today the Earl and Countess of Wessex's home. Louise bore Arthur, Margaret and Patricia. Arthur was another born soldier, Margaret died whilst pregnant in 1920 and Patricia renounced her H.R.H. when she married Alexander Ramsey in 1919.

Prince Arthur of Connaught accidently shot Prince Christian his favourite sister Helena's husband, in the eye whilst out for a day's sport, and he was forgiven. Christian had a range of false eyes made which he liked to show to his guests at dinner parties. Arthur outlived all his siblings, except Beatrice.

Leopold George Duncan Albert, 1853-1884. Victoria first used chloroform during this childbirth and she keenly advocated its qualities. Leopold was diagnosed as a haemophiliac, so he had to be careful not to injure himself; a trip or fall could lead to extensive blood loss, pain, and in the worst case, his death. Victoria tried to cosset, if not control him. She portrayed her youngest son as a tragic angel to be pitied, whilst he wanted to live life to the full. Her journals frequently refer to *poor little Leopold*. He was intelligent, a keen reader and academic, receiving praise from luminaries including Alfred, Lord Tennyson, the Poet Laureate. After a persistent campaign by Leopold, Victoria allowed him to study at Christ Church, Oxford University from 1872-1876 where he befriended and romanced Alice Liddell, the inspiration for another friend, Charles Lutwidge Dodgson's, literary work using the pen name of Lewis Carroll, Alice's Adventures in Wonderland.

Leopold left university with an honorary degree in civil law.

He was created Duke of Albany, Earl of Clarence and Baron Arklow in 1881. On 27th April 1872 Leopold married Helena of Waldeck-Pyrmont at St. George's Chapel, Windsor and they had two children, Alice in February 1883 and Charles in July 1884, four months after his father's haemophilia related death in Cannes, France on 28th March.

Beatrice Mary Victoria Feodore, or Baby, was born in 1857. After Prince Albert's death in 1861 Baby became the focus of Queen Victoria's grief. Whilst the queen's other daughters found freedom by marrying and passing the care of their mother and unofficial private secretary duties to the next in line, the queen assumed that her youngest child, shy and loyal Beatrice, would be her devoted companion until death.

When Beatrice stated her wish to marry Queen Victoria refused to talk to her for six months. She eventually relented, on the condition that Beatrice and the new husband, Prince Henry of Battenberg, known as Liko, would remain in her household.

The couple married in July 1885; independence through marriage and motherhood to four children, 3 boys and a girl, was difficult to achieve; Beatrice was enslaved to her mother's whims and demands on her time.

In January 1896 Liko died of malaria whilst on a military expedition in Africa during the Ashanti War.

Baby was responsible for editing Queen Victoria's journals after the queen's death. She led a largely private life but appeared at the cenotaph frequently from 1921 to lay a wreath on 11th November, Armistice (Remembrance) Day. She died in her sleep on 26th October 1944 aged 87.

Queen Victoria and "Baby" circa 1862.

60. In 1840, after the death of Princess Augusta, the second daughter of George III and Queen Charlotte, Victoria gave her mother the use of Clarence House in London and Frogmore House at Windsor.

61. Victoria was a firm believer in getting fresh air, even in the middle of winter. No matter how inclement the weather, the queen was

rarely dissuaded from taking a carriage excursion, a walk or going riding.

62. Victoria survived seven assassination attempts during her reign. In 1840, Edward Oxford fired two pistols at the pregnant queen, she was uninjured. Oxford was declared insane and sent to Broadmoor Hospital in Berkshire. On 30th May 1842, John Francis' gunshot missed the queen in her carriage on The Mall, outside Buckingham Palace. He was swiftly apprehended. He had intended to harm Victoria on the 29th May, but he either lost his nerve or his gun misfired as he stood on The Mall. The 1842 Treason Act was introduced, and Francis was sentenced to death, this was commuted to transportation. One month after Francis' attempt, John W. Bean fired a gun filled with paper and clay piping, but his shots missed Victoria, Albert and their guest, Leopold, King of the Belgians as they journeyed between St. James' Palace and the Chapel Royal in London. Bean was eventually arrested and sentenced to 18 months in prison because although the materials

released from the weapon were not lethal, the paper could have set the queen's dress on fire. William Hamilton fired a blank towards Victoria's carriage in 1849. He alleged that he intended no harm to the monarch, that he was destitute and believed that whilst in prison he would at least eat properly and have a roof over his head. He was charged with a misdemeanour towards the monarch and was sentenced to seven years transportation. Another regicide attempt was made in 1850. Robert Pate, an ex-army officer, managed to injure Queen Victoria whilst she was sat in a phaeton. He struck her with an iron cane and she was left with a black eye, a bleeding wound and scarring. Her bonnet was smashed on impact. She defiantly attended the opera that evening sporting her black eye and in pain. She was hailed as a hero; Pate received a sentence of seven years transportation. In 1872 Irishman Arthur O'Connor waited around the grounds of Buckingham Palace; he wanted to persuade the queen to free every Irish prisoner held in Britain. O' Connor aimed a pistol at her face as she left her carriage, but he was overpowered and arrested before he could do any serious harm. He was duly sentenced to one year in prison and 20 strikes with the birch. Newspaper reports stated that the queen was unaffected by the event but privately she considered that this attempt on her life *at home* was the most frightening. It was the first attempt on her life since Prince Albert's death. Roderick Maclean made the last assassination attempt in 1882. A vagrant and poet, he was motivated to challenge the queen after she returned some of his poetry with less than glowing praise. He became fixated with her. (He also hated the number 4.) Maclean shot at Victoria at Windsor railway station. He was tried for treason, found to be insane and therefore not guilty. The queen was dissatisfied with the verdict and a change in the law followed; "guilty but insane" came into use alongside the term used during Maclean's case: "not guilty by reason of insanity."

63. Victoria was the first monarch to travel by train. She achieved this on 13th June 1842 with Prince Albert as they made their journey

from Slough (near to Windsor Castle) to Paddington Station in London. Victoria was "charmed" by this mode of transport. The Industrial Revolution had transformed the country in the early 1800's and railways were extensively built throughout Victoria's reign to replace canal transportation networks, increasing speed and efficiency. In 1869 Victoria had a purpose-built luxurious carriage made, intended for royalty only. In 2017 restoration work was carried out on the ornate carriage.

64. Whilst maintaining Buckingham Palace in London, which Prince Albert considerably modernised, and historic but gloomy Windsor Castle as their homes, they added Osborne House on the Isle of Wight in 1845 and Balmoral Castle in Aberdeenshire, Scotland in 1852 as privately owned, not crown, properties. Osborne House was designed by Prince Albert and built by Thomas Cubitt, an ancestor of Camilla, Duchess of Cornwall, in the Italianate palazzo style. He had already added the front wing to Buckingham Palace

which hosts the balcony. Osborne took seven years to complete and was largely funded by selling the spectacular Brighton Pavilion and its contents. The pavilion was built and furnished by the Prince Regent. Osborne House featured a private beach, the Swiss Cottage which housed a functional kitchen and gardens for the children, ornate public rooms and homelier royal apartments. Albert had Balmoral Castle rebuilt less than 100 metres from the original castle between 1852 and 1856. With its granite stone and baronial turrets, set in 50000 acres of stunning landscape, it reminded Albert of the Thüringen Forest in which he'd grown up. A bridge was built from the castle to the nearby village of Crathie and the royal family would often visit their tenants and the vulnerable in the area, acting as normally as royalty ever can.

65. The Irish Famine (*Gorta Mór*) of 1845-1849 led to over one million deaths and a similar number of emigrations. It was primarily caused by potato blight and exacerbated by absentee landowners. Victoria found that as

Ireland's ruler she was angrily referred to as The Famine Queen. In 1847 she made the largest single donation, £2000, to the aid fund. It was a myth created by disaffected Irish Nationalists that she only gave £5 to the famine relief and that she donated the same sum to the Battersea Dogs Home in London. It was not until 1849 that she made her first visit to Ireland, after resentment to the authority in London had ebbed a little but even today the famine, and the period under British rule, remain contentious issues in Ireland.

66. The Great Exhibition of 1851 was held at the newly built and magnificent Crystal Palace which was designed by architect and botanist Joseph Paxton. Prince Albert and Henry Cole organised the exhibition, the first international event of its kind, staged to exhibit British craftsmanship and industry alongside the best of its global competitors' products. Victoria and Albert co-ordinated the grand opening ceremony on 1st May 1851. There were 14000 exhibitors from 25 countries and approximately 6 million people

visited the Great Exhibition between 1st May and its final day, the 15th October 1851. That represented 1/3 of the British population. The event had its critics, Victoria's uncle, the Duke of Cumberland, ruling in Hanover, wrote to a friend about the "folly and absurdity" of Victoria allowing the exhibition to take place. Victoria wrote in her journal: *"This day is one of the greatest & most glorious days of our lives, with which, to my pride & joy the name of my dearly beloved Albert is for ever associated!"* The South Kensington museums in London: The National History Museum, Victoria and Albert Museum and the Science Museum were built using the proceeds.

67. The Victoria Cross was created in 1856, in response to acts of valour carried out by Victoria's military subjects. At the time, the Crimean War against Russia was in its final days and Britain's ally France had the Legion d'honneur to reward bravery. Britain required a similar honour. The "V.C." displayed the highest level of recognition from the monarch to a subject, alive or posthumously, for valour

in the face of the enemy. It had (and has) no class or ethnicity distinctions. The Victoria Cross is set beneath a crimson ribbon (blue for naval recipients.) It features a bronze cross pattée with a crown and lion image and "For Valour." Victoria made the first awards in June 1857 and the metal used to make the medals was believed to have been sourced from Russian weaponry at the Siege of Sevastopol. Recipients were often nominated by their fellow military service personnel.

The Crystal Palace's front entrance, 1851.

The Victoria Cross.

68. Victoria may have been the world's most powerful woman, but she couldn't understand why women would want rights, particularly the right to vote. The notion made her furious. *"The Queen is most anxious to enlist everyone in checking this mad, wicked folly of "Women's Rights.""*

69. She never said, "We are not amused." Her granddaughter Alice of Athlone (Prince

Leopold's daughter) was confident of this when asked about the phrase most commonly associated with Victoria. However, Queen Victoria was often amused and had an enthusiastic loud laugh. Footage of the queen at her diamond jubilee (1897) shows her smiling broadly.

70. In 1857 parliament agreed that Victoria could bestow the title of Prince Consort to Prince Albert as a sign of recognition for his dedication and work towards the Empire's prosperity. He is the only official Prince Consort to a British queen in Britain's history. Being a Prince Consort does not offer the same status as a king or the consort's spouse, the Queen.

71. Victoria's mother, Victoire, Duchess of Kent died on the morning of 16th March 1861. *"She breathed her last, my hand holding hers to the last moment."* Victoria had Albert to thank for a reconciliation between mother and daughter; he had worked hard to improve Victoria's understanding of the Duchess. In her grief Victoria realised that her mother had

always loved her, and that precious time had been wasted in anger.

72. Prince Albert died in the Blue Room at Windsor Castle on 14th December 1861. Typhoid Fever was blamed. Albert's poor health, agonising stomach pains, the increase in duties caused by Victoria's consuming grief for her mother and Bertie's dalliance with Nellie Clifden contributed to the 42 years old's inability to overcome the fever. Victoria's last journal entry for 1861 was written on the 13th December when signs of recovery gave hope.

73. Victoria blamed Bertie for Albert's death and could barely tolerate being in the same room. She sent him on an overseas tour so that she wouldn't be forced to see him for several months. Albert had suggested in the last weeks of his life that Bertie should marry to calm him down; Victoria was determined that upon his return home Bertie would find a wife. Princess Alexandra of Denmark was recommended by Vicky from Prussia, Bertie was ambivalent, but he and Alix were married

on 10th March 1863 at St. George's Chapel, Windsor. The queen wore black and stayed out of sight during proceedings. Photographs of the newlyweds stood either side of a grim-faced Queen Victoria as she gazed at a large bust of Prince Albert were taken.

The Widow at Windsor

74. After Albert's death Victoria wore black and forbade any jewels but diamonds as being too frivolous. From the 1870's she often wore her widow's veils with a small and light diamond crown that she had created so she would appear regal in person and in images, and always in mourning for Albert.

75. Albert's first floor rooms at Osborne House on the Isle of Wight were preserved as they were when he last visited in the summer of 1861, as if he would somehow return to them at any moment. His clothes were laid out and fresh water placed in the room each morning for decades. Even today, when these rooms have long been open to the public, they appear as they did over 150 years ago.

76. The queen was consumed with grief and she had no wish to carry out public duties. Ensconced in a life of sad seclusion, often at beloved Balmoral or Osborne House, she could rarely be persuaded to visit London.

For several years she continued with her private constitutional tasks like the red boxes from parliament, remained interested in European events and kept a fierce hold on her children's behaviour but because the public couldn't see her doing anything, republicanism increased in popularity.

77. Some historians have suggested that the severity of her grief and its longevity signal that Victoria suffered from porphyria, the disease which is widely believed to have afflicted her grandfather, George III. Certainly, George portrayed signs of mental illness and mania and Victoria's depression can be used to link the two.

78. She finally bowed to pressure and appeared in public after someone attached a notice to the gates of Buckingham Palace in March 1864: "These commanding premises to be let or sold in consequence of the late occupant's declining business."

79. It was 1866 before she attended the annual State Opening of Parliament. This is a

ceremony which reaffirms the relationship between the monarch, the House of Lords and the House of Commons. Prior to Prince Albert's death she had frequently attended the opening; processing to Westminster where she made a speech outlining the plans for the coming parliamentary year whilst wearing the regalia. After 1866 she was present at just six more State Openings of Parliament in the remaining thirty-four years of her reign.

80. The small diamond crown she was often shown wearing as a widow was created for two reasons: The weighty Imperial State Crown gave her headaches and she wanted a more comfortable solution. Her small diamond crown sat perfectly on her lace mourning veils, portraying the required image of a mourning monarch. She first wore the small crown for the State Opening of Parliament on the 9th February 1871. The design was believed to have been inspired by Queen Charlotte's Nuptial Crown which was used in Hanover from 1870. Although Victoria's small diamond crown was a

personal possession, she left it to the crown in her will, so it was occasionally used by queen consorts, Alexandra and Mary, wives of Edward VII and George V. Today, Victoria's crown is kept in the Jewel House at the Tower of London.

81. Extracts from her journals were published in the late 1860's and early 1870's under the titles, "*Leaves from the Journal of Our Life in the Highlands.*" And "*More Leaves from the Journal of Our Life in the Highlands.*"

82. Victoria became increasingly fond of and dependent on John Brown, a hard drinking, plain speaking Scottish servant originally based at Balmoral. He was born in 1826, the second of eleven children and he worked as a farm labourer before gaining employment at Balmoral in the years before Victoria and Albert bought it. Prince Albert suggested that Brown should be given the task of guiding Victoria's pony when they ventured out, and he was promoted to Albert's personal ghillie in 1849. In December 1864 he was made a full-time servant at all of Victoria's homes;

her daughter Alice had noted that the queen seemed content when out on her pony and with John Brown for company. Most of Victoria's children refused to tolerate Brown's brusqueness and insubordination; Victoria adored his directness. By 1866, rumours were circulating that Brown and Victoria were lovers, that they secretly married and even that the queen bore a secret child. She was frequently referred to by satirists as Mrs Brown. She created two honours for him: A Faithful Servant medal and the Devoted Service medal.

83. On 28th March 1883 John Brown died. A desolate Victoria recorded in her journal that she had not only lost a servant but a real friend. Brown had caught a chill but refused to take time off; when he finally agreed to rest it was too late to save his health. He was buried at Crathie Kirk, close to Balmoral. Devotion to duty, and Victoria, may well have killed him.

84. A popular name attributed to Victoria was The Widow at Windsor; in 1890, Rudyard

Kipling (1865-1936) wrote a poem with the title "Sons of the Widow." It was republished in 1892 as "The Widow at Windsor" in the first section of Barrack-Room Ballads. The widow in the piece was Queen Victoria.

85. Victoria made an error when she chose not to believe that John Brown's younger brother Archie, to whom she had given the role of personal valet to Prince Leopold, habitually ill-treated him verbally and physically. He made Leopold's life a misery. Leopold wrote about Archie Brown hitting him with spoons; for a haemophilia sufferer Archie's actions could easily have had grave consequences. In spring 1866, Lieutenant Walter George Stirling of the Household Artillery was employed as Leopold's governor and when he was suddenly dismissed after four months it raised questions. The official reason for his departure was that a more experienced governor for her delicate son was necessary, but rumour had it that the teenaged Princess Louise was worryingly smitten and too familiar with Stirling.* With the speed of his dismissal there was no official replacement

and Archie Brown, a bully who abused his position, was temporarily given the task. After a complaint from another member of the household, Archie was demoted but not dismissed. (*Some historians and claimants believe, but have not yet conclusively proved, that Louise had a son by Stirling.)

86. Benjamin Disraeli (1804-1881) was a favourite Prime Minister, probably because he knew that by using charm he could get the outcome or answer he wanted. He believed that, "Everyone likes flattery and when you come to royalty you should lay it on with a trowel." He did this expertly. A two-time Prime Minister, novelist, reformer and orchestrator of Victoria's elevation to Empress of India, Disraeli was rewarded by Queen Victoria in 1879; he was created 1st Earl of Beaconsfield.

87. Less fortunate was four-time Prime Minister William Ewart Gladstone (1809-1898) who she felt spoke to her as if she was, "a public meeting rather than a woman." A politician since the age of 23, his last election as Prime

Minister in 1882 and his tenure until resignation in 1884 are both records in the history of British politics: The oldest Prime Minister to form a government and the oldest Prime Minister to occupy the role. A public sign of Victoria's dislike for Gladstone was made on his retirement when she decided not to bestow a title on him, as was customary, because she was sure that he would not want it. He had refused an earldom earlier in his career and it suited her not to approach him on the subject again.

88. The Royal Titles Act was passed in 1876 so that Victoria could assume the title of Empress of India in 1877. India was already under British rule and a Governor General represented the queen there. The elevation to Empress of India from queenship was to raise Victoria to the same rank as the Tsar of Russia and Wilhelm I in Germany. Wilhelm I's government had rewarded him with the German emperorship after victory in the Franco-Prussian war and so on 1st January 1871 he became the *Deutscher Kaiser*. Piqued at being of a lower status than other rulers,

Victoria first stated her wish to be an empress in 1873 whilst Gladstone was Prime Minister; it took a change to Disraeli as leader and "An Act to enable Her most Gracious majesty to make an addition to the Royal Style and Titles appertaining to the Imperial Crown of the United Kingdom and its Dependencies." to deliver her prize: "Her Majesty Victoria, by the Grace of God, of the United Kingdom of Great Britain and Ireland Queen, Defender of the Faith, Empress of India." Robert Bulwer-Lytton, 1st Earl of Lytton was the incumbent Governor General and his title was altered to Viceroy of India and Governor General.

89. Fascinated by India, Victoria had two Muslim servants brought to the UK in summer 1887, Mohamed Abdul Karim and Mohamed Baksh; the ornate Durbar Room at Osborne House was designed by Lockwood Kipling, the father of Rudyard, in the early 1890's. Once introduced to curries, they became a welcome meal for Victoria.

90. Mohammed Abdul Karim was born in Lalitpur near Jhansi in India in 1863. At

court, he was known as the Munshi (teacher.) Soon after his arrival he became Victoria's favourite servant and she made him her Indian Secretary, gave him honours – Commander of the Victorian Order and Companion of the Most Eminent Order of the Indian Empire - and awarded him a parcel of land in Agra, India. As much as Victoria favoured him, her family and the court were less impressed. They found the Munshi arrogant and made no secret of their dislike of his being a foreigner. Her relatives and the household were astonished when the queen insisted that at events the Munshi should not eat with the servants, as was normal, but with her guests. Victoria ensured that he was schooled in the English language and he taught the queen Urdu and Hindustani. When Victoria died, Edward VII had Karim sent back to India and there he lived quietly until his death, aged 46.

91. Victoria's Golden Jubilee, for 50 years as monarch, was held on 20th June 1887. The government co-ordinated a celebration that was to reach to the far corners of the empire;

she was then the longest reigning monarch in history and some of her subjects had been born and died in the Victorian era. She offered continuity, rather like Elizabeth II does today. Victoria had not had a Silver Jubilee because it fell soon after Prince Albert's death when she was keen to stay out of the public eye. On 20th June 1887 the family gathered at Frogmore House at Windsor to commemorate her accession to the throne. Later, Victoria travelled to London Paddington railway station where she was met by cheering crowds and decorated streets. There was a banquet at Buckingham Palace that evening. On the 21st June there was a service of thanksgiving at Westminster Abbey which was attended by family, heads of state, officials from around the globe and honoured guests. On the procession to the Abbey, soldiers, including the Indian Calvary, escorted Victoria in her landau. A Te Deum composed by Prince Albert was included in the service. That evening, bonfires were lit around the country. On 22nd June the Queen visited "The Children's Jubilee" for approximately 27000 at Hyde Park, London.

Each child received a jubilee mug as a keepsake. She returned to Windsor Castle with an escort. Abdul Karim and Mohamed Baksh became servants on 23rd June 1887, and another children's party was held, for 6000, at Home Park at Windsor. A Buckingham Palace Garden Party was organised for the 29th June and huge crowds watched the queen arrive at the palace after her journey from Windsor. She returned to the seclusion of Windsor that evening. One of the last Golden Jubilee engagements took place at Osborne House at the end of July; a farewell to the Indian princes who had attended the celebrations.

92. Victoria's Diamond Jubilee in June 1897 was the first time that diamond was used to describe 60 years duration. Her jubilee coincided with the Festival of the British Empire and she had to be persuaded that a public celebration of her reign was necessary. A bank holiday was proclaimed. Street parties, free ale and cigarettes were donated by wealthy philanthropists. As her mobility was becoming restricted, and she had no wish

to totter (or fall) up or down the steps at St. Paul's Cathedral she insisted that the thanksgiving service was preached outside so that she could remain in her carriage.

Queen Victoria's official Diamond Jubilee photograph. 1897.

93. Queen Elizabeth II became Britain's longest reigning monarch on 9th September 2015. Prior to this Queen Victoria held the record, reigning for 63 years and 216 days. Interestingly, a pretender to the throne, the Catholic James Stuart (The Old Pretender) would have had a reign of 64 years, 3 months and 16 days if he had been officially recognised, thereby eclipsing Victoria's record.

94. Victoria Day – Fete de la Reine or Celebration of the Queen - was first held in Canada in 1845 to celebrate her birthday. A law was passed in 1901 to ensure that the day would be known as Victoria Day and in 1952 the date was secured as the Monday closest to her birthday between 18th-24th May inclusive. It is a state holiday. Today, Victoria Day celebrates Elizabeth II's official birthday.

95. Victoria had planned her burial in detail. She would have a military funeral and be laid to rest beside Prince Albert at the Frogmore Mausoleum at Windsor, dressed in white. Beside her in the coffin lay Prince Albert's

dressing gown, a cast of his hand and some photographs. Her discreet physician, Dr. James Reid, pulled her wedding veil down over her face. Reid was left in charge of the coffin until it was sealed which gave him the opportunity to secretly place a lock of John Brown's hair, the Scotsman's photograph and a ring that his mother had owned alongside Victoria. Reid wrapped and covered them with flowers so that the royal family would not see them.

96. As she was laid to rest beside Albert in the mausoleum, it started to snow. Only Victoria and Albert were ever laid to rest in that building. She had intended it to be a shrine to her beloved husband and it was built and consecrated in 1862. Victoire, Duchess of Kent has her own mausoleum at Frogmore and some other royals rest in the nearby Royal Burial Ground, including Victoria and Albert's son and daughter, Arthur and Louise, Edward VIII and Princess Victoria, the 2nd daughter of Edward VII and Queen Alexandra.

97. Victoria's last Prime Minister was Robert Gascoyne Cecil, 3rd Marquess of Salisbury. He did not long survive the queen, he passed away on 22nd August 1903, aged 73. He is buried in the churchyard of St. Etheldreda's Church in Hatfield, Hertfordshire, so is Lord Melbourne, Victoria's first Prime Minister; he passed away on 24th November 1848.

98. Her nine children produced forty-two grandchildren and they populated most of the European royal houses. By the end of the First World War several of them had been deposed, exiled or had been assassinated. Most of the living ex-German, Greek, Austrian and Russian royals were disillusioned by the loss of "the old order." Victoria and Albert's vision of a British-Prussian led peaceful continent, that started with their daughter Victoria's marriage to Friedrich of Prussia came to nothing; not that they, or anyone else, could have imagined the Great War and its carnage.

99. King Edward VII ascended to the throne in 1901. Victoria was called the Grandmama of

Europe, and he was regarded as the "Uncle of Europe." He was a natural diplomat. Whilst alive, he managed to ensure his relatives sustained peace. When he died, so too did lasting hopes of peace between nations. Victoria would never have thought that her son would have had such a positive impact.

100. Edward VII had Victoria's beloved statue of John Brown moved to a discreet corner of the Balmoral estate.

101. Edward VII gifted Osborne House to the state; this was directly against his mother's wishes, but he had no wish to live there. Today it is managed by English Heritage and open to the public. From 1903-1921 the grounds housed a Royal Naval College; a convalescent home for officers was opened during World War I and closed in the 1990's. In 1954 Queen Elizabeth II allowed Victoria and Albert's suites to be opened to the public. In 2012 the private beach was made available to visitors.Upon their mother's death, Edward VII instructed his sister Beatrice to edit their mother's multi-volume journal entries so that

nothing which could cause a scandal or be misconstrued remained. Consequently, a lot of the journal entries we see today are in Beatrice's handwriting and edited in accordance with Victorian and Edwardian sensibilities. In 2016, a slice of Queen Victoria and Prince Albert's wedding cake from 1840 sold at auction for £1500. Presented in a box with the wording, "The Queen's Bridal Cake Buckingham Palace, Feby 10, 1840." A sheet of paper bore the queen's signature. At the same auction, a pair of her drawers with drawstring waist showing a crown image and her initials fetched over £16000. In 2012 one of her mourning outfits sold for £6200, three times the estimate. Each of these items is proof that we're still fascinated by Queen Victoria and the age that she ruled over.

The End.

Printed in Great Britain
by Amazon